COOKING WITH YOUR KIDS

Sandra Rudloff

BRISTOL PUBLISHING ENTERPRISES
San Leandro, California

A nitty gritty® Cookbook

Printed in the United States of America.

ISBN: 1-55867-250-8

Cover design: Frank J. Paredes
Cover photography: John A. Benson
Food stylist: Susan De Vaty
Illustrations: Pam Johnson

CONTENTS

Acknowledgments

A giant thank-you to my sons, Jonathan and Stephen, for helping me, critiquing me, and inspiring me. And of course, thank you to my husband Chris, who put up with all the food experiments and the pots that created them.

COOKING WITH YOUR KIDS

Kids in the kitchen can be a dream come true, or a nightmare. My children, boys aged 6 and 7, love to help out in the kitchen. They are much more willing to try new foods when they have helped to make them; and they love the praise from Daddy and Mommy about how good their cooking is.

TIPS

Each recipe for *Cooking with Your Kids* was created in our home kitchen, with the help of Jonathan and Stephen. Before you begin cooking with your child, here are a few thoughts to keep in mind:

Relax your expectations. You need to be a bit more relaxed in your expectations of the final dish. It doesn't matter if the carrot chunks aren't exactly uniform in size. It doesn't matter if the cake has too much frosting on one side. What really does matter is that you allow your children to learn, play and experiment. If you are too exacting, they won't enjoy it, and you can easily hurt their feelings.

Cutting, scooping, measuring, mixing. These are the most fun for kids to do. Little ones love to scoop and measure. Let your kids do all the cutting or chopping, and all the measuring and mixing unless otherwise noted. There are cases where you should do the cutting, such as cutting meat and using a sharp knife.

Take your time. If you are in a time crunch, it probably isn't a good idea to have the kids help a lot. One of my sons is very precise when cutting vegetables. I factor this in when I ask for his help.

Be creative. Many of the recipes in this book came directly from ideas that Jon and Stephen came up with. They learned how to take their favorite foods and combine them in different ways. So what if they want to try dipping chicken chunks into applesauce — it might just be tasty!

Supervise, supervise, supervise. I have a set of knives for my boys — they are fairly dull serrated knives that can still do the job of cutting vegetables. But I always stay with them, and always watch over their shoulder to make sure they are using the tools correctly. Even though the knives aren't very sharp, they can still cut through skin if dragged across a finger.

ADULTS AND KIDS MAKE BREADS AND BREAKFASTS

BANANA MUFFINS

These are like individual banana breads.

3 ripe bananas, mashed
1 cup sugar
1 egg
1/4 cup vegetable oil
1/2 cup applesauce
2 1/4 cups flour
2 tsp. baking soda

Adult: Heat oven to 300°. Spray a 12-cup muffin pan with nonstick spray.

Kids: In a large bowl, stir bananas, sugar, egg, oil and applesauce until well mixed. Add flour and baking soda and stir just to mix. Scoop batter into muffin cups equally.

Adult: Place muffin pan in oven and bake for 30 minutes. Cool in pan for 5 minutes; remove muffins to a wire rack to cool completely.

CHOCOLATE CHIP MUFFINS

This is our favorite way to eat chocolate in the morning. They also make a great afternoon snack.

2 cups all-purpose flour
1 tbs. baking powder
$\frac{1}{2}$ tsp. salt
$\frac{1}{2}$ tsp. baking soda
$\frac{2}{3}$ cup sugar

2 eggs
1 cup buttermilk
$\frac{1}{4}$ cup butter, melted and cooled
$1\frac{1}{2}$ tsp. vanilla extract
1 cup chocolate chips

Adult: Heat oven to 350°. Spray a 12-cup muffin pan with nonstick spray.

Kids: In a medium bowl, stir together flour, baking powder, salt, baking soda and sugar. In a separate bowl, mix together eggs, buttermilk, butter and vanilla. Add liquid to flour mixture and stir lightly. Add chocolate chips and stir only enough to mix. Spoon batter into muffin cups equally.

Adult: Place muffin pan in oven and bake for 20 to 25 minutes, or until muffins are light golden brown. Remove from oven and cool for 5 minutes in pan; remove to a wire rack to cool completely.

WHITE CHOCOLATE CHERRY MUFFINS

Don't think these are too sophisticated for your family's taste — they are sweet and chewy, and remind my family of cherry vanilla ice cream.

1³/₄ cups all-purpose flour
1 tsp. baking soda
¹/₄ tsp. salt
¹/₂ cup butter
1 cup sugar
1 cup buttermilk
1¹/₂ tsp. vanilla extract
1 egg
2 oz. white chocolate, melted and cooled
¹/₂ cup dried cherries, chopped
¹/₂ cup white chocolate chips

Adult: Heat oven to 350°.

Kids: Line a 12-cup muffin pan with paper muffin liners.

In a medium bowl, stir flour, baking soda and salt together until well mixed. Set aside. In another bowl, with an electric mixer on low speed, cream butter and sugar together until very light, about 5 minutes. Add egg and melted white chocolate and mix until smooth. In another bowl, mix buttermilk and vanilla.

Pour half of the flour mixture into butter mixture and beat until smooth. Pour in ½ cup buttermilk and mix again; add remaining flour and mix. Add remaining buttermilk, dried cherries and white chocolate chips, and beat until well mixed. Spoon batter equally into muffin cups.

Adult: Place pan in oven and bake for 25 to 30 minutes. Cool in muffin pan for 5 minutes; remove from pan to a wire rack to cool completely.

CINNAMON MUFFINS

Makes 12

These are wonderful on a fall morning; they are delicious with a glass of cold milk, a cup of tea, or my personal favorite, a tall latte.

2 cups all-purpose flour
2/3 cup brown sugar, packed
1 tbs. baking powder
1/2 tsp. salt

1 tbs. ground cinnamon
1 egg
1 1/2 cups buttermilk
1/3 cup butter, melted

Adult: Heat oven to 400°.

Kids: Line a 12-cup muffin pan with paper muffin liners.

In a large bowl, combine flour, brown sugar, baking powder, salt and cinnamon. With your fingers, mix ingredients together.

In another bowl, mix together egg, buttermilk, and butter. Pour liquid mixture over flour mixture and stir just until blended. Spoon batter equally into muffin liners.

Adult: Place pan in oven and bake for 20 minutes, or until a toothpick inserted in the center comes out clean. Remove from oven and let muffins cool in pan for 5 minutes. Serve warm, or cool completely and store.

CRANBERRY MUFFINS

You can make these a day ahead of a big meal; just store tightly wrapped (or in a plastic bag) in the refrigerator.

$3/4$ cup apple juice
$3/8$ cup vegetable oil
1 egg
$3/4$ cup sugar

1 cup chopped cranberries
$13/4$ cups all-purpose flour
1 tbs. baking powder
$1/4$ tsp. salt

Adult: Heat oven to 400°. Spray a 12-cup muffin pan with nonstick spray.

Kids: In a large bowl, combine apple juice, oil, egg and sugar. Mix well. Add cranberries and stir to mix. In another bowl, stir together flour, baking powder and salt. Add flour mixture to apple juice mixture and stir just to mix. Do not overmix. Scoop batter into muffin cups by $1/4$ cupfuls.

Adult: Place pan in oven and bake for 20 to 25 minutes, or until muffins are light golden brown. Remove from oven and cool in pan for 15 minutes. Remove from pan and serve warm, or cool completely and store in refrigerator.

CRAZY CRAISIN SCONES

Makes 8

Craisins are dried, sweetened cranberries. You can find them year-round in the supermarket where raisins are sold.

1/4 cup butter
1 3/4 cups all-purpose flour
1/4 cup sugar
1 tbs. baking powder
1/2 tsp. salt
1/2 cup buttermilk
1 egg
2 tsp. vanilla extract
1/2 cup craisins

Adult: Heat oven to 425°. Spray an 8-inch round cake pan with nonstick spray. Melt butter in a small saucepan and cool slightly.

Kids: In a medium bowl, mix together flour, sugar, baking powder and salt. In another bowl, mix together melted butter, buttermilk, egg, vanilla and craisins. Stir well to mix. Pour liquid mixture over flour mixture and stir to make a stiff dough.

Place dough on a lightly floured surface and knead about 10 times. Place dough in an 8-inch round cake pan. With your fingers, press dough to cover bottom of pan in an even layer.

Adult: With a pizza cutter or a fork, cut dough into 8 wedges. Place pan in oven and bake for about 15 minutes, or until scones are light golden brown. Cool for 10 minutes and serve warm with plenty of butter and jam.

Family Food Tip: Take breakfast outdoors! Have a picnic breakfast, or just eat in your backyard for a fun start to your weekend.

APPLE COFFEECAKE

Servings: 8-10

The finely chopped apples in this cake add flavor and moisture.

2 Granny Smith apples
1 tsp. cinnamon
1/2 cup butter
1 cup sugar
1 cup sour cream
2 eggs
2 cups flour
1 tsp. baking powder
1 tsp. baking soda
1 cup confectioners' sugar
1/2 tsp. vanilla extract
4 tsp. water

Adult: Peel and core apples. Spray a tube pan or Bundt pan heavily with nonstick spray. Heat oven to 350° (325° if using a dark-coated pan).

Kids: Finely chop apples. Combine chopped apples and cinnamon in a small bowl and stir to mix. Set aside.

In a large bowl, with an electric mixer, cream butter and sugar together until smooth. Add sour cream and eggs, and beat on medium speed until well mixed, about 3 minutes.

In another bowl, stir together flour, baking powder and baking soda. Add dry ingredients to butter mixture and mix well. Add apples and stir just to mix into batter. Scoop batter into prepared pan.

Adult: Place pan in oven and bake for 45 to 55 minutes, or until a toothpick inserted in the cake comes out clean. Cool in pan for 10 minutes; invert pan onto a wire rack, remove pan and let cake cool.

Kids: In a small bowl, mix together confectioners' sugar, vanilla and water. Stir until smooth. Drizzle over cooled cake.

CRUNCHY GRANOLA

If your family likes almonds or other nuts, add ¹/₂ cup when you are mixing the oats with the other ingredients.

¹/₄ cup honey
¹/₄ cup vegetable oil
2 tbs. apple juice concentrate
1 tsp. cinnamon
2 tbs. brown sugar
2 cups old-fashioned oats
¹/₂ cup toasted wheat germ
¹/₂ cup coconut
1 cup raisins

Family Food Tip: Instead of offering your kids the same things every morning for breakfast, write down the possibilities on a piece of paper, like a menu, and let them place their order. They have to pay for the meal, as in a restaurant, but with hugs and kisses!

Adult: Heat oven to 300°. Spray a large cookie sheet with nonstick spray.

Kids: In a small saucepan, combine honey, oil, apple juice concentrate, cinnamon and brown sugar.

Adult: Place saucepan over medium heat until sugar has dissolved and mixture is smooth. Remove from heat and cool until you can stick your finger in mixture comfortably.

Kids: In a large bowl, combine oats, wheat germ and coconut. Stir to mix. Pour cooled honey mixture over oats, and use your hands to mix until all ingredients are well coated. Spread mixture evenly on a large cookie sheet.

Adult: Place cookie sheet in oven and bake for 30 minutes. Stir and return to oven to continue baking for another 30 minutes or until lightly browned. Remove from oven and cool. Stir in raisins. Store in an airtight container for up to 2 weeks.

BLUEBERRY BREAKFAST CAKE

Servings: 8

If your family likes blueberry muffins, they will love this cake. It is best served warm from the oven, with a dollop of butter on each piece.

1 egg
2/3 cup milk
1/4 cup sugar
2 tbs. butter, melted
2 cups buttermilk baking mix

1 cup fresh or frozen blueberries, thawed if frozen
1 tbs. buttermilk baking mix
2 tbs. brown sugar, packed

Adult: Heat oven to 400°. Spray a 9-inch square baking dish with nonstick spray.

Kids: In a large bowl, mix together egg, milk, sugar and butter. Stir well to blend. Add 2 cups baking mix and stir only to moisten. Batter should be lumpy. Add blueberries and stir gently to mix. Pour batter into prepared pan. In a small bowl, mix together remaining 1 tbs. baking mix and brown sugar. Sprinkle sugar mixture over batter.

Adult: Place pan in oven and bake for 20 to 25 minutes, or until cake is light golden brown. Remove from oven and cool in pan for 15 minutes. Serve warm.

LUMBERJACK OATMEAL PANCAKES
Servings: 4 (about 12 pancakes)

These hearty pancakes are a great way to start an active fall or winter day. Try topping them with hot cinnamon apples or applesauce instead of maple syrup.

1/2 cup all-purpose flour
1/2 cup quick-cooking oatmeal
1 cup buttermilk
1 tbs. sugar
2 tbs. vegetable oil
1 tsp. baking powder
1/2 tsp. baking soda
1/2 tsp. salt
1 egg

Adult: Heat a pancake griddle while kids mix pancakes.

Kids: Using an electric mixer on low speed, beat all ingredients until smooth. Pour 1/2 cup batter onto hot griddle (have your adult help you!). Cook until puffed and dry around the edges, flip over and cook the other side until golden brown.

APPLE STRATA

If your family likes cinnamon apples and French toast, they will love this break-fast dish. It is a cross between French toast, custard and a Dutch baby pancake, and is a great fall or winter brunch dish. This should be assembled the day before for best results. Serve it with maple syrup, if you like.

1/4 cup butter
2 Golden Delicious apples, peeled, cored and sliced
1/2 tsp. cinnamon
3/4 cup sugar, divided
8 slices white bread
6 eggs
3 cups milk

Adult: Spray a 9-x-13-inch baking dish with nonstick spray. In a large skillet, melt butter over medium heat. Add apples and stir to coat with butter. Sprinkle cinnamon and $1/4$ cup sugar over apples and stir to mix. Sauté until apples are tender, but not breaking down, about 4 minutes. Remove from heat and cool.

Kids: Place bread in baking dish, overlapping slices if necessary. In a medium bowl, mix together eggs, milk and $1/2$ cup sugar, beating until well mixed. Pour egg mixture over bread. Spoon apples and any liquid in pan evenly over egg mixture. Cover tightly with plastic wrap and put in refrigerator overnight, or for at least 4 hours.

Adult: Heat oven to 425°. Remove plastic wrap from baking dish and place dish in oven. Bake until a knife inserted in the center comes out clean, about 35 to 45 minutes. Serve hot.

Family Food Tip: Self-serve breakfast! Friday night, help your small kids to put dry cereal and raisins into locking plastic bags, and pour milk and juice into spill-proof containers. Set the beverages on a low shelf in your refrigerator, and set the snack bags on the counter. Program the TV to a favorite station for Saturday morning cartoons. When the kids get up Saturday morning, breakfast is waiting — and you can enjoy a few more minutes of shut-eye.

PARMESAN BREAD RING

Makes 1 loaf

Of course, if you have the time and desire, you can make your own bread dough. But it so easy to use frozen bread dough, that I try to keep some on hand.

1 loaf frozen white bread dough
1/2 cup butter, melted
1/2 tsp. dried oregano

1/2 tsp. dried basil
1/2 cup grated Parmesan cheese

Adult: Defrost dough according to package directions. Spray a 10-inch tube or Bundt pan with nonstick spray.

Kids: Combine butter, oregano and basil in a small bowl. Pull off a golf-ball-sized chunk of bread dough, dip it into butter-herb mixture and roll it in Parmesan cheese. Place in prepared pan. Continue with all dough, layering it in the pan as you go. Put pan in a warm place and let dough rise until almost double.

Adult: Heat oven to 375°. Place bread in oven. Bake for 25 to 30 minutes, or until it sounds hollow when lightly tapped. Remove from pan, and cool on a wire rack at least 15 minutes before serving. To serve, either cut into slices, or let your family pull off pieces.

PITA CHIPS

Makes 72 pieces

These chips are great for scooping up heartier dips and spreads. They also make a great base for appetizer toppings.

6 pita breads
2 tbs. vegetable oil
1 tbs. seasoning salt

Adult: Heat oven to 350°. Cut pita breads into 3 wedges each.

Kids: Peel pita bread halves apart. Place pitas, smooth-side down, on a baking sheet. Lightly brush tops with vegetable oil and sprinkle with seasoning salt.

Adult: Place baking sheet in oven. Bake for about 12 to 15 minutes, or until crisp. Cool and serve as you would crackers or chips.

ADULTS AND KIDS MAKE
SOUPS AND SALADS

CREAMY VEGETABLE SOUP

The great thing about this soup is that the vegetables used are pretty much family favorites, and the vegetables are available fresh year-round.

2 cans (14½ oz. each) chicken broth
2 large russet potatoes, peeled and
   chopped
1 cup chopped carrots
1½ cups frozen corn kernels

1 cup chopped celery
1½ cups chopped zucchini
1 tsp. salt
1 cup milk

Kids: Combine chicken broth and potato in a large soup pot or Dutch oven.

Adult: Bring mixture to a boil over high heat. Cover, reduce heat to low and simmer for 15 minutes, or until potato is very soft. Remove potato from broth and place in a blender container. Pulse until pureed; return puree to chicken broth.

Kids: Add carrots and corn to broth. Stir to mix.

Adult: Bring to a boil over medium heat, reduce to low and cook until carrots are tender-crisp, about 5 to 10 minutes.

Kids: Add celery and zucchini to soup. Stir to mix.

Adult: Cook until vegetables are tender, about 5 more minutes. Add milk and serve.

MEATBALL MINESTRONE

*Use the recipe for **Tender Meatballs** on page 62 — this is a filling soup for cold winter days, and goes perfectly with lots of hot garlic bread.*

1 lb. cooked meatballs
½ yellow onion, chopped
2 cans (14½ oz. each) beef broth
1 stalk celery, chopped
1 small zucchini, chopped
1 cup shredded napa cabbage
½ cup chopped carrots

1 can (28 oz.) ready-cut tomatoes
1 can (8 oz.) kidney beans, rinsed and
    drained
½ tsp. salt
½ tsp. dried basil
½ tsp. dried oregano
½ cup broken angel hair pasta, uncooked

Kids: Combine all ingredients except angel hair pasta in a large soup pot or Dutch oven.

Adult: Bring soup to a boil over high heat. Cover, reduce heat to low and simmer for 15 minutes. Remove lid and return to a full boil over high heat. Add pasta and cook according to package instructions. Serve as soon as pasta is tender.

HAM AND POTATO SOUP

Servings: 6-8

This soup is a great way to use up leftover ham. It also freezes well.

3 cups water
2 cups chicken broth
5 large potatoes, peeled and chopped
3 stalks celery, sliced
2½ cups chopped ham
1 tsp. salt
2 cups milk

Kids: In a large soup pot, combine water, broth and potatoes.

Adult: Bring mixture to a boil, reduce heat to low and simmer until potatoes are very tender, about 30 minutes. Remove 2 cups of the potatoes from broth. Place in a blender or food processor container and pulse until smooth. Return puree to pot.

Kids: Add celery, ham and salt to soup.

Adult: Simmer soup until celery is tender, about 15 minutes. Add milk and continue to heat on low until very hot, but not boiling.

PUMPKIN CURRY SOUP

Servings: 8

Pumpkin cooks up just like any other squash. This is a mild, smooth soup, and just slightly flavored with curry. My kids enjoy pulling out the "pumpkin guts." It's fun to keep the seeds and roast them later.

1 pumpkin, 3-4 lb.
3 cups chicken broth
2 large russet potatoes, peeled and cubed
1 tsp. curry powder
1 cup half-and-half

Family Food Tip: Let your kids choose the meal for one night each week. You can let them choose from a few items, but let them decide for the whole family.

Adult: Cut top off pumpkin, enough for hands to fit in easily.

Kids: Scoop out all seeds and loose fibers, using a spoon to help.

Cut pumpkin into chunks and peel.

Kids: Place pumpkin, broth and potatoes in a large soup pot. Bring mixture to a boil, cover and reduce heat to low. Simmer for 45 minutes, or until pumpkin and potatoes are tender.

Adult: Remove pumpkin and potatoes to a blender or food processor. Pulse until smooth, adding broth if needed. Return to soup pot.

Kids: Add curry powder to soup. Bring soup to a boil.

Adult: Remove from heat. Add half-and-half and salt to taste. Serve immediately.

MEXICAN POTATO CHEESE SOUP

Creamy potato soup gets a lift from mild green chiles and rich cheddar cheese (medium or sharp). Add a green salad and some cornbread, and you have a complete meal.

½ yellow onion, chopped
2 stalks celery, thinly sliced
1 clove garlic, minced
1 can (4 oz.) chopped mild green chiles
1½ lb. red-skinned potatoes, cut into
   large chunks

2 cups chicken broth
½ tsp. salt
½ cup half-and-half
1 cup shredded cheddar cheese

Kids: In a large soup pot, combine onion, celery, garlic, chiles, potatoes, chicken broth and salt.

Adult: Bring soup to a boil over medium heat, cover and reduce heat to low. Simmer for 30 minutes, or until potatoes are very tender. Scoop out about 2 cups of the potatoes with a bit of liquid. Pulse in blender container until pureed, and return to pot. Bring mixture to a boil over medium heat; add half-and-half and cheese. Reduce heat to low and stir until cheese has melted and soup is hot. Do not allow to boil. Serve immediately.

ANGEL HAIR SOUP

The first thing my boys asked about this recipe was "where do angels get their hair cut?" This is simply a different version of chicken noodle soup.

5 cups chicken broth
2 carrots, peeled
2 stalks celery, thinly sliced
4 oz. dried angel hair pasta

Kids: Pour chicken broth into a large pot. Cut carrots into large chunks.

Adult: Place pot on stove, and over high heat, bring to a boil. Cover and reduce heat to low. Simmer until carrots are very soft, about 20 to 30 minutes, depending on size of chunks. Remove carrots to a strainer or sieve.

Kids: Using the back of a spoon, press carrots through strainer and into broth. Continue to press and scrape until all carrots have been pushed through. Add celery to broth.

Adult: Bring broth to a full boil, and add pasta. Cook according to package directions, about 3 to 5 minutes. Remove from heat and serve.

EGG FLOWER SOUP

Everyone always goes "Oooooh," when they see the eggs float back up in the soup. This is fun to make, and an easy way to start an Oriental meal.

4 cups chicken broth
1 tbs. soy sauce
¼ cup slivered water chestnuts
½ cup thinly sliced celery
3 eggs, beaten

Kids: In a large saucepan, mix together broth, soy sauce, water chestnuts and celery.

Adult: Heat chicken broth mixture to boiling over high heat. Reduce heat to low.

Kids: With the help of your adult, slowly pour egg into broth. Count slowly to ten, and then gently stir soup. The egg "flowers" will float to the top when they are cooked.

FRUIT SALAD WITH HONEY DIP

Servings: 6-8

Skewer the fruit pieces onto bamboo skewers, and serve little cups of the dip alongside.

½ cup honey
1 cup vanilla-flavored yogurt
1 can (16 oz.) pineapple chunks
3 apples, cored and cut into chunks
2 cups red and/or green grapes
2 bananas, peeled and sliced
2 cups strawberries, halved

Kids: Combine honey and yogurt in a small bowl. Cover and refrigerate for 30 minutes.

Combine all fruit in a large serving bowl, or skewer on sticks if desired. Serve salad or fruit skewers, and pass dip separately.

Family Food Tips: When you shop for produce, let children choose a fruit or vegetable — the only condition is that they eat what they choose.

COLONEL'S LADY SALAD

We have no idea why this salad has its name — but it is pretty and bright green.

DRESSING

¾ cup mayonnaise
1 tbs. chopped fresh parsley
1 tbs. chopped chives
¾ tsp. tarragon
1 tbs. white vinegar

SALAD

1 head iceberg lettuce, torn into bite-sized pieces
1 cup frozen peas, thawed
1 cucumber, peeled and thinly sliced
1 stalk celery, thinly sliced

Kids: Place dressing ingredients in a blender container. Pulse until smooth and light green in color. Remove from blender and refrigerate.

In a salad serving bowl, combine lettuce, peas, cucumber and celery. Toss to mix. Add half of the dressing and toss to mix. Add additional dressing if desired. Serve immediately.

TIGER SLAW

My boys think of tigers when they see the "stripes" of carrot in this salad. This is a sweeter, crunchier slaw than regular cole slaw. It also doesn't have a really strong cabbage flavor, which a lot of kids dislike. If your children are old enough, let them shred the cabbage and carrots.

3 cups shredded cabbage
2 apples, cored and chopped
1½ cups shredded carrots
½ cup mayonnaise
1 tsp. lemon juice
1 tbs. sugar
½ tsp. salt

Kids: Combine all ingredients in a large bowl. Toss to mix, cover and refrigerate for 30 minutes before serving.

Family Food Tip: Give foods silly names. Children will usually try something new if it has a funny name.

TEX-MEX THREE-BEAN SALAD

Servings: 6-8

Everyone has had enough of plain three-bean salad, with its sweet dressing. This zesty salad is bright and colorful, and has a mildly spicy dressing.

1 can (15 oz.) black beans
1 can (15 oz.) pinto beans
1 can (15 oz.) green beans
2 cups chopped celery
1 ½ cups corn, canned or frozen and thawed
1 can (4 oz.) chopped olives
½ cup vegetable oil
½ cup vinegar
½ tsp. garlic salt
½ tsp. ground cumin

Kids: Rinse and drain all beans. Place in a large bowl. Add all remaining ingredients and stir to toss. Cover and refrigerate for at least 4 hours before serving. Mix again before serving.

TACO SALAD DRESSING

You can use this on your lettuce salads, as a vegetable dip, or even top your tacos.

1 pkg. (1.25 oz.) taco seasoning mix
2 cups sour cream
1 cup mild salsa or picante sauce

Kids: Mix all ingredients together, cover and refrigerate for 1 hour. Stir before using.

Family Food Tip: Let the "props" sell what you are serving. Collect a variety of placemats or colorful dishes to make a change from the same old thing.

ADULTS AND KIDS MAKE
FISH, POULTRY AND VEGETARIAN ENTRÉES

CLASSIC MAC AND CHEESE

Servings: 6-8

I used to think my kids were addicted to that little blue box — but I broke their habit when we began making our own. Experiment with the cheese until you find one you like. And we love to change pasta shapes. Our favorite is fusilli, or corkscrew pasta, because the sauce really sticks to the spirals.

¼ cup butter
¼ cup flour
4 cups milk
3 cups shredded cheddar cheese
1 lb. pasta shapes, cooked per package directions

Adult: In a large saucepan, melt butter over medium heat. Add flour, and using a wire whisk, stir until smooth. Add milk, stirring constantly with whisk, and cook over medium heat until thickened, about 10 minutes. Remove from heat.

Kids: Add shredded cheese and stir with a spoon until cheese has melted. Add cooked pasta and stir gently to mix.

BAJA FISH TACOS

Servings: 4-6

You won't find these at Mexican fast food restaurants, but authentic Mexican restaurants usually have them on the menu. Use your family's favorite type of fish fillet, such as cod, red snapper or halibut, but make sure it is boneless.

1 lb. fish fillets
½ tsp. salt
¾ tsp. ground cumin
¼ tsp. black pepper
¼ tsp. paprika
2 tbs. butter, melted
1 tbs. lemon juice
flour tortillas

OPTIONAL ADDITIONS
salsa
shredded lettuce
sour cream
shredded cheddar cheese
chopped olives

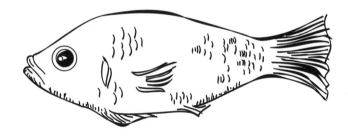

Adult: Heat oven to 400°. Cut fish into bite-sized chunks, about 1-inch square. Spray a baking sheet with nonstick spray.

Kids: In a large plastic bag, combine salt, cumin, pepper and paprika. Add fish pieces and shake to coat. Place fish in a single layer on baking sheet. Drizzle melted butter over fish.

Kids: Place 12 tortillas on a sheet of foil. Cover with another sheet of foil, and fold edges.

Adult: Place fish and foil-covered tortillas in oven. The fish will cook very quickly, so check often, beginning at 5 minutes, and test by inserting a fork in the center of a chunk; it is done when it flakes and the center is opaque. When done, remove from oven and place in a warm serving bowl. Squeeze lemon juice over fish and toss to coat. Let your family assemble their own soft tacos.

CRISPY OVEN-FRIED FISH

My kids love fish sticks, so it was easy to get them to try these crispy fish fillets. Serve with your favorite cole slaw for a super fast dinner.

2 lb. cod fillets
½ cup plain yogurt
¼ cup vegetable oil
¼ cup yellow cornmeal
¼ cup dry unseasoned breadcrumbs
2 tbs. all-purpose flour
½ tsp. salt
¼ tsp. pepper

Adult: Cut fish into serving pieces, if necessary. Place an oven rack in the top position of oven. Heat oven to 500°. Spray a baking dish with nonstick spray. The dish should be big enough to accommodate all fish in a single layer without crowding.

Kids: Place yogurt in a shallow plate. Add fish and turn over once to coat. Leave fish in yogurt while oven heats, turning over every few minutes.

Adult: When oven temperature has reached 500°, pour 2 tbs. oil on the bottom of baking dish and heat for 5 minutes. Have kids finish preparing fish while oil heats.

Kids: On a plate, mix together cornmeal, breadcrumbs, flour, salt and pepper. Remove fish from yogurt and let excess drip off. Place fillets on cornmeal mixture and press lightly to get crumbs to adhere to all sides of fish. As you finish a fillet, set it aside and continue until all have been coated.

Adult: Remove baking dish from oven. Place coated fillets in hot oil, being careful not to splatter. Drizzle remaining oil over fish, and return dish to oven. Bake for about 8 minutes, or until opaque in the center. Remove fish to a paper towel to drain slightly and serve immediately.

SEASHORE SHELLS AND SHRIMP

Servings: 4-6

The creamy sauce in this pasta dish helps to mellow the taste of the shrimp — it is a great way to introduce your children to shrimp.

1 cup heavy cream
$\frac{1}{2}$ lb. cooked bay shrimp
$\frac{1}{2}$ tsp. salt
12 oz. pasta shells, cooked per package directions and drained
$\frac{1}{2}$ cup grated Parmesan cheese

Adult: In a large saucepan, heat cream over medium heat.

Kids: Add shrimp and salt to cream and remove from heat.

Adult: Pour hot cream mixture over hot cooked pasta.

Kids: Sprinkle Parmesan over sauce. Using two large spoons, gently toss pasta and sauce to evenly coat pasta and to distribute Parmesan cheese.

CHICKEN "RISOTTO"

Risotto is often served as a side dish, or as the pasta course. Here the addition of chicken and vegetables make a filling and homey entrée.

¼ cup butter
2 yellow onions, minced
2 cups Arborio rice
1 cup chopped white mushrooms

8 cups chicken broth
2 cups chopped cooked chicken
1 cup green peas, thawed if frozen
½ cup grated Parmesan cheese

Adult: In a large pot, melt butter over medium heat. Add onion and rice and sauté until onion is translucent, about 5 minutes.

Kids: Carefully add mushrooms, broth and chicken.

Adult: Increase heat to high and bring mixture to a boil. Reduce heat to low, cover and simmer for 20 minutes, or until rice is just tender. Remove from heat.

Kids: Add green peas and Parmesan, stirring to mix. Cover and let stand for 5 minutes before serving.

CREAMY CHICKEN AND PASTA

Servings: 4-6

This is total "comfort food." Serve with warm bread or rolls for a complete meal in a bowl. It is also delicious with cooked turkey.

¼ cup butter
½ cup all-purpose flour
2 cups chicken broth
2 cups milk
½ tsp. salt
3 cups coarsely chopped cooked chicken
1 cup coarsely chopped celery
1 cup green peas
8 oz. uncooked rotini, fusilli, wagon wheels
   or other pasta shape

Adult: In a large saucepan, melt butter over medium heat. Add flour, and using a wire whisk, mix thoroughly. Add chicken broth, milk and salt, and whisk until smooth. Heat mixture over medium heat, stirring constantly until thickened, about 10 minutes. Remove pan from heat.

Kids: Very carefully add chicken, celery and green peas to saucepan. Stir to mix.

Adult: Reduce heat to low and return pan to heat. Cover and simmer while you prepare pasta. Cook pasta according to package directions and drain when done. Put pasta in a large warm serving bowl, and pour chicken and sauce over pasta. Serve immediately.

EARTHQUAKE CHICKEN NUGGETS

Servings: 4-6

My kids love to "shake it up" when we make this — it is even more fun if you put on some good dancing music, and REALLY shake it up!

3 boneless, skinless chicken breast halves
2 eggs
1 cup milk
1½ cups Italian-seasoned breadcrumbs
2 cups prepared spaghetti sauce, warmed

Adult: Heat oven to 450°. Spray a baking sheet with nonstick spray.

Kids: Place a chicken breast in a plastic food bag. Using a kitchen mallet, pound chicken to a ¼- ½-inch thickness. Remove chicken from bag and repeat with other breasts.

Adult: Cut pounded chicken into 2-inch pieces.

Kids: Mix eggs and milk together. Put all chicken into milk mixture and stir. Leave in milk mixture for 5 minutes.

Place breadcrumbs in a large plastic food bag. Take a piece of chicken from milk mixture and let excess drip off. Place about 5 pieces into bag with breadcrumbs. Seal bag (use a twist tie or use a locking plastic bag) and shake it until chicken pieces are completely coated in breadcrumbs. Remove chicken from bag and place on prepared baking sheet. Continue until all chicken has been coated in breadcrumbs.

Adult: Place baking sheet in oven and bake for about 5 minutes. Turn nuggets over and bake for another 5 minutes, or until golden brown. Remove from oven and cool for a few minutes before serving. Pass warm sauce with chicken for dipping.

BISCUIT TURKEY POT PIE

Servings: 4-6

If you like pot pies, but don't want to bother with making pie crust, here is an easier way to do it. It is topped with biscuit dough, and tastes great. It is also a good way to use up holiday turkey or leftover chicken meat.

¼ cup plus 1 tbs. butter, divided
1 cup chopped fresh mushrooms
½ cup chopped yellow onion
½ cup chopped carrots
½ cup chopped celery
½ cup frozen green peas
2 cups diced cooked turkey
¼ cup flour
1½ cups chicken broth
½ cup milk
½ tsp. salt

BISCUITS
1 cup buttermilk baking mix
⅓ cup milk

Adult: Melt 1 tbs. butter in a medium saucepan over medium heat. Add mushrooms and onions and sauté until they begin to brown, about 5 minutes. Put mushroom and onion mixture into a 2-quart casserole dish. Heat oven to 425°.

Kids: Add carrots, celery, green peas and turkey to casserole dish and stir to mix.

Adult: In the medium saucepan you used before, melt ¼ cup butter over medium heat. Sprinkle in flour and stir with a wire whisk until smooth. Add broth, milk and salt, stirring constantly to keep lumps from forming. Heat until just boiling and mixture is thick. Pour mixture over turkey and vegetables. Stir to mix and place in oven. Bake for 25 minutes.

Kids: In a small bowl, combine baking mix and ⅓ cup milk. Stir until smooth.

Adult: At the end of 25 minutes, remove casserole dish from oven. Carefully spoon biscuit dough on top of vegetables and turkey. Return to oven and bake for another 10 to 15 minutes, or until biscuits are lightly browned. Serve immediately.

HONEY-GRILLED CHICKEN

A quick marinade in the grilling sauce makes the chicken tender and sweet. This is good with any cut of chicken. Just adjust the cooking time if using larger pieces.

½ cup honey
¼ cup water
¼ cup catsup
4 boneless, skinless chicken breast halves

Kids: In a shallow plate or baking dish, stir together honey, water and catsup. Place chicken in marinade. Marinate for 30 minutes, turning once.

Adult: Prepare a medium-hot grill or broiler. Remove chicken from marinade, letting excess drip off. Reserve marinade. Cook chicken for about 4 to 5 minutes per side, basting frequently with marinade. If desired, heat marinade in a small saucepan over high heat and bring to a boil. Boil for 2 minutes and serve with chicken.

SPANISH CHICKEN

If your family likes Spanish rice, they will like this chicken dish, flavored with the same ingredients. Try serving on top of hot white rice.

2 tbs. olive oil
1 chicken, cut into pieces
2 cans (14½ oz. each) ready-cut tomatoes
1 yellow onion, chopped
1 green bell pepper, seeded and chopped
2 tsp. ground cumin
2 tsp. seasoning salt

Adult: Heat oil in a large skillet over medium heat. Add chicken and brown on all sides.

Kids: Carefully add tomatoes, onion, green pepper, cumin and seasoning salt. Stir gently to mix. Cover tightly with lid.

Adult: Return skillet to stove and simmer on low for about 20 minutes, or until chicken is tender.

MOM'S FAVORITE VEGETABLE PIE

Servings: 4-6

One of my boys loves this, and of course, the other doesn't. But it is my favorite vegetable pie because I love spinach and broccoli. You really do need to use frozen vegetables for this recipe, because you can squeeze or drain off excess liquid — otherwise, if you use fresh vegetables, this will not bake correctly.

1 pkg. (10 oz.) frozen chopped
   spinach, thawed and squeezed dry
1 pkg. (10 oz.) frozen chopped
   broccoli, thawed and drained
4 eggs

½ cup milk
4 strips cooked bacon, chopped
1½ cups shredded cheddar cheese
1 tsp. salt
1 deep dish pie crust, unbaked

Adult: Heat oven to 375°.

Kids: In a large bowl, combine all ingredients except pie crust. Mix very well. Pour mixture into pie crust.

Adult: Wrap edges of crust in aluminum foil to prevent excess browning. Place pie in oven and bake for 50 to 60 minutes, until firm. Remove from oven and cool for 5 minutes before serving.

ADULTS AND KIDS MAKE MEAT ENTRÉES

PINEAPPLE PORK CHOPS

Servings: 4

This is a mild version of teriyaki pork. You can also barbecue chops if you prefer.

4 pork chops, about 1-inch thick
¼ cup brown sugar, packed
2 tbs. soy sauce
½ cup pineapple juice

Adult: Trim as much excess fat from chops as possible. Set aside.

Kids: In a shallow bowl, combine brown sugar, soy sauce and pineapple juice. Stir until brown sugar dissolves. Add pork chops and turn to coat both sides of chops with marinade. Place in the refrigerator. After 15 minutes, turn chops over in marinade for 15 minutes more.

Adult: Heat oven to 400°. Remove chops from marinade, reserve marinade and place chops in a shallow baking pan. Bake for about 45 minutes, or until tender. Baste frequently with reserved marinade. Remove from oven and serve immediately.

PORK CHOPS WITH MUSHROOM SAUCE

Servings: 6

Even if your kids don't like mushrooms, they will like this sauce. You can easily remove the mushrooms, and still have plenty of sauce for their chops.

2 tbs. butter
6 pork chops, about 1-inch thick
½ lb. sliced mushrooms

1 tbs. flour
1½ cups beef broth
½ cup sour cream

Adult: Melt butter in a large skillet over medium heat. Add chops and cook until browned, about 5 to 7 minutes on each side. Remove chops from pan.

Kids: Add mushrooms to skillet. Stir to loosen up any brown bits on bottom of skillet. Cook mushrooms uncovered over low heat until they release moisture.

In a small bowl, mix together flour and beef broth until smooth. Pour beef broth mixture over mushrooms.

Adult: Bring mixture to a boil over high heat, stirring frequently. Boil on high for about 10 minutes to reduce sauce, stirring frequently. Reduce heat to low and return chops to skillet. Simmer pork chops in sauce until done. Remove from heat and stir in sour cream until smooth. Place chops on a warm serving platter and top with sauce. Serve immediately.

WATERMELON RIBS

The watermelon juice marinade makes the ribs moist and tender. It's also a lot of fun to squish out the juice!

3 cups fresh squeezed watermelon juice
½ cup catsup
2 tbs. soy sauce
5 lb. pork spare ribs, cut into 2-rib sections

Kids: Squeeze pieces of ripe watermelon with your hand to extract juice. Strain juice and discard any pulp or seeds. Pour juice in a large glass baking dish. Add catsup and soy sauce and stir to mix. Place ribs in marinade and turn ribs to cover all sides with marinade. Cover and place in the refrigerator for 4 to 8 hours, stirring occasionally.

Adult: Heat oven to 325°. Drain marinade from pan and reserve. Place ribs in oven and roast uncovered for 1½ hours, basting occasionally with reserved marinade.

TINY TEXAN RIBS

These are fun to eat because they are so small! They also make a great, but a bit messy, appetizer for parties. Marinating the meat not only makes it more tender and juicy, but also gives it a sweet flavor throughout.

3 lb. pork ribs
½ cup catsup
¼ cup brown sugar
2 tbs. apple cider vinegar

1 tbs. Worcestershire sauce
¼ cup apple juice
¼ cup honey

Adult: Have your butcher cut ribs into 2-inch pieces. Cut racks into individual ribs.

Kids: Combine all ingredients in a large locking plastic bag (you may need to use 2 bags). Place bags on a plate and refrigerate for 3 hours to marinate. Turn bags over once halfway through time to distribute marinade.

Adult: Heat oven to 325°. Spray the bottom and sides of a 9-x-13-inch baking dish or a cookie sheet with 1-inch sides with nonstick spray.

Kids: Pour ribs and marinade into prepared baking dish.

Adult: Place dish in oven and bake for 1½ hours, stirring occasionally. Remove from oven and remove ribs with a slotted spoon. Serve immediately.

CHILE COLORADO

True chile Colorado has quite a bit of fire to it — here is a recipe that is flavorful, but not hot. Pass the Tabasco sauce when you serve this, and let everyone decide how much fire they can take.

2 lb. beef stew meat
2 tbs. vegetable oil
1 yellow onion, minced
2 cloves garlic, minced
1 tsp. ground cumin
1 tsp. paprika
1 can (14½ oz.) beef broth
3 tbs. tomato paste
½ tsp. salt

Adult: Cut beef into bite-sized pieces. In a large pot, heat oil over medium-high heat. Add beef and brown well on all sides. Remove from heat.

Kids: Add onions and garlic to pot and stir to mix.

Adult: Continue to cook over medium-high heat, until onions are translucent. Remove pot from heat.

Kids: Add cumin, paprika, beef broth, tomato paste and salt. Stir well until mixed.

Adult: Return pot to heat and bring to a boil. Reduce heat to low, cover and simmer for about 3 hours, or until beef is fork-tender. Remove lid during last 30 minutes to help reduce sauce. Serve hot.

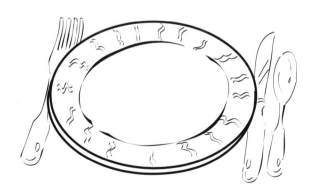

MEATBALLS OLÉ

Serve this entrée with warm flour tortillas or some Spanish rice. Be sure to use you family's favorite salsa or picante sauce — don't try something too hot and spicy the first time you make this!

1 lb. lean ground beef
¼ cup dried breadcrumbs
1 egg
½ cup water
1 pkg. (1.25 oz.) taco seasoning mix
2 cups salsa or picante sauce
½ cup shredded cheddar cheese

Adult: Spray a cookie sheet with nonstick spray.

Kids: In a large bowl, mix ground beef, breadcrumbs, egg, water and taco seasoning (you can use your hands for this). When thoroughly mixed, cover and put in the refrigerator for 15 minutes to allow flavors to blend. Scoop out about 2 tablespoons of the mixture and shape into a meatball. Place meatballs on prepared cookie sheet.

Adult: Heat oven to 350°. Place meatballs in oven and bake for 20 to 25 minutes, or until meatballs begin to brown. Remove meatballs from pan and set aside. Prepare a 9-inch square baking dish by spraying bottom and sides with nonstick spray.

Kids: Pour 1 cup of the salsa into baking dish. Place all meatballs on sauce, in two layers if necessary. Pour remaining salsa over meatballs and top with shredded cheddar cheese.

Adult: Place dish in oven and bake for 15 to 20 minutes at 350°, or until salsa is bubbling and cheese has melted. Remove from oven and cool for 5 minutes before serving.

TENDER MEATBALLS

Makes about 20

While my son Jon and I were rolling the meatballs, he asked if he could make meat squares, or meat triangles. He even made some meat snakes! Let your kids have fun making different shapes. These are called tender because they are softer than typical meatballs; consequently, you bake rather than fry them. You can use these in your favorite spaghetti, or in meatball sandwiches, or any other recipe where you use meatballs.

1 lb. lean ground beef
1/3 cup dried breadcrumbs
1 egg
2 tbs. water
2 tbs. catsup
1 tbs. Worcestershire sauce
1/4 tsp. salt
1/4 tsp. dried basil
1/4 tsp. dried oregano

Adult: Heat oven to 350°. Spray a cookie sheet with nonstick spray.

Kids: In a large bowl, mix all ingredients (you can use your hands for this). When thoroughly mixed, scoop out about 2 tablespoons of the mixture and shape into meatballs, or any other shape. Place meatballs on prepared cookie sheet.

Adult: Place pan in oven and bake for 20 to 25 minutes, or until meatballs begin to brown. Remove from oven and cool slightly. Remove from pan and use as desired (or cool completely and freeze for future use).

BEEF CHOW MEIN

Servings: 4

It's a running joke in my family, that whenever we have "a big dish of beef chow mein," we howl. It's a werewolves of London thing...

1 pkg. (6 oz.) chow mein stir-fry noodles*
1 tsp. vegetable oil
½ yellow onion, sliced
1 cup thinly sliced beef
2 stalks celery, sliced
2 cups thickly sliced cabbage
1 zucchini, sliced
1 cup beef broth
1 tbs. soy sauce
2 tsp. cornstarch
2 tbs. water
¼ tsp. garlic salt

* You can usually find these noodles in the Asian foods section of most supermarkets. You can also use the same amount of buckwheat noodles, Chunka Soba noodles or angel hair pasta.

Adult: Prepare noodles according to package directions. Drain and keep warm. While water boils for noodles, begin meat and vegetables. In a large wok, heat oil over high heat. Add onion and beef, and cook until beef is done, about 4 minutes.

Kids: Add celery, cabbage, zucchini, beef broth and soy sauce to wok. Stir to mix. Let mixture come to a boil.

In a small bowl, mix together cornstarch, water and garlic salt.

Adult: Add cornstarch mixture to boiling meat and vegetables, stirring constantly. Cook until vegetables are tender-crisp, about 2 minutes. Add cooked noodles and toss to mix. Serve immediately.

THIEVES' BEEF STEW

Servings: 4-6

One evening, my family asked for beef stew — at 4:30 PM! No time to make an all-day stew in my slow cooker, so I made this. It is called "thieves'" stew because I stole the gravy from a package of instant beef mushroom gravy, and also because I "stole" the time it normally takes to cook stew. This works best if you use a better cut of meat than standard stew meat; since you aren't cooking it very long, you need tender beef to begin with. I like to use a cut called tri-tip. Feel free to change the vegetables, depending on your family favorites. Serve with pasta, mashed potatoes or rice (the gravy is great on top of egg noodles!).

2 tbs. vegetable oil
2 lb. beef sirloin tip or other good cut
water
1 pkg. (1 oz.) beef gravy mix
1 cup sliced carrots
¾ cup sliced celery
½ cup green peas, frozen or canned

Adult: Heat oil over medium-high heat in a Dutch oven or large pot. Add beef and brown well on all sides.

Kids: In a medium bowl, according to beef gravy package directions, mix together water and gravy mix. Pour mixture into Dutch oven and stir well.

Adult: Cover Dutch oven and reduce heat to medium-low. Simmer for 15 minutes, stirring frequently.

Kids: Add carrots and celery to meat. Stir to mix. Cover and cook until meat and vegetables are tender, about another 15 to 25 minutes. One or two minutes before serving, add peas and stir to mix. Serve when peas are hot.

SLOW-COOKED POT ROAST

Servings: 8

Slow-cooked eye of round becomes fork-tender. The juices make a rich gravy, perfect on top of hot mashed potatoes.

1 boneless beef eye-of-round roast, about 3 lb.
1 tbs. vegetable oil
1 cup beef broth
½ yellow onion, chopped
1 tsp. dried rosemary
½ tsp. dried thyme
2 cloves garlic, minced
1 tbs. Dijon mustard
2 tbs. cornstarch
3 tbs. water

Adult: Trim beef of any visible fat. Heat oil over medium-high heat in a skillet large enough to accommodate meat. Add beef and brown well on all sides.

Kids: Place the following ingredients into the Crock-pot® or slow cooker: beef broth, onion, rosemary, thyme, garlic and mustard. Stir to mix. Place browned beef in pot and turn over once. Cover and set slow cooker on low heat. Cook for 9½ to 10½ hours.

Adult: Remove beef from pot, place on a serving platter and keep warm. Pour all cooking liquid from slow cooker into a medium saucepan. Blend cornstarch and water together until smooth. Bring cooking liquid to a boil over medium heat and add cornstarch, stirring constantly. Bring to a boil, reduce heat to low and cook for an additional 3 minutes. Serve gravy with roast.

PARISIAN-STYLE SHORT RIBS

These ribs have all the flavors of French onion soup. Quartering the onions makes them easy to remove if you have someone who doesn't like them.

2 tsp. vegetable oil
3 lb. beef short ribs
2 yellow onions, peeled and quartered
1 can (14 oz) beef broth

2 tbs. Worcestershire sauce
1/4 cup sherry
1/4 tsp. salt

Adult: Heat oven to 350°. Heat a large skillet or Dutch oven over medium-high heat. Add oil and short ribs and brown ribs on all sides. Place browned ribs in a 9-x-13-inch baking dish or a large covered casserole dish.

Kids: Put onion on top of beef. In a large bowl, mix together broth, Worcestershire sauce, sherry and salt. Pour liquid over beef and onions. Cover tightly with foil or with a lid.

Adult: Place dish in oven and bake for 2½ hours, or until meat is fork-tender. Remove meat and onions from pan and place on a serving dish. Skim fat from sauce, and serve sauce with ribs.

WALK-AWAY BEEF STEW

You don't even have to brown the meat first. You can throw everything together in less than 10 minutes, and then come back to a complete meal.

3 carrots
2 russet potatoes
2-2½ lb. beef stew meat
1 clove garlic, minced
1 yellow onion, chopped
1 tbs. Worcestershire sauce

1½ cups beef broth
¼ cup tomato paste
¼ tsp. salt
½ tsp. dried basil
1 tsp. sugar

Adult: Peel carrots and potatoes.

Kids: Cut carrots into 2-inch pieces. Cut potatoes into large chunks, about the size of the carrot chunks. Put all ingredients into a slow cooker and stir to mix well.

Adult: Cover and set slow cooker on high temperature. Return in 6 hours, stir, and serve.

HERBED LONDON BROIL

London Broil is delicious grilled or broiled. The herb butter that is poured over the sliced meat is mild and a bit Italian-tasting.

1 London broil, about 1-2 lb.
2 tsp. seasoning salt or garlic salt
½ cup butter
1 tsp. dried basil
1 tsp. dried oregano
½ tsp. dried rosemary
½ tsp. salt
¼ tsp. black pepper

Family Food Tip: Set aside (or buy) a "special" plate and use it to honor a family member (including parents) for a special effort or achievement. Perhaps Jake won a spelling bee — or Mary made her bed 7 days in a row — or Mom or Dad got a raise. Dinner on the blue plate!

Adult: Prepare a hot grill or preheat the broiler.

Kids: Sprinkle 1 tsp. of the seasoning salt on each side of meat. In a small saucepan, place butter and all other ingredients.

Adult: Place meat on hot grill or under broiler. Cook to desired doneness, about 7 minutes on each side for medium. While meat is cooking, heat butter and herbs in a saucepan over medium heat. When butter has melted, reduce heat to low to keep butter very warm. Remove meat from grill and let stand for 5 minutes before cutting.

Thinly slice meat against the grain and place on a warm serving plate. Drizzle hot herbed butter over meat and serve.

ADULTS AND KIDS MAKE
SIDE DISHES

CHEESY POTATOES

Parmesan is not meant just for pasta! The mild nutty cheese bakes with potatoes and milk for a special version of a favorite potato dish.

2 lb. potatoes, about 6 medium, washed and peeled if desired
1 1/4 cups shredded Parmesan cheese
1/2 tsp. ground nutmeg
1 tsp. salt
1 1/2 cups milk

Adult: Heat oven to 400°. Cut potatoes into 1/4-inch slices.

Kids: Place about 1/3 of the potatoes on the bottom of a 2-quart casserole dish. Sprinkle 1/2 cup of the Parmesan over potatoes. Place another 1/3 of the potatoes in the dish, topping with 1/2 cup of the Parmesan. Place remaining potatoes on top.

In a small bowl, mix together nutmeg, salt and milk. Pour mixture over top of potatoes. Sprinkle remaining 1/4 cup Parmesan on top.

Adult: Place casserole in oven. Bake for 1 hour, or until potatoes are tender. If top browns too quickly, cover with foil. Remove from oven and let stand for 10 minutes before serving.

OVEN-BAKED BROWN RICE WITH MUSHROOMS

Servings: 4-6

Next time you make a beef roast, try this instead of pasta or noodles. It is really flavorful and moist, and goes very well with most beef entrées.

8 oz. fresh white mushrooms
¼ cup butter
½ cup minced yellow onion
1 cup long-grain brown rice
2¼ cups beef broth
¼ tsp. salt

Kids: Wash mushrooms and chop coarsely. Set aside.

Adult: Heat oven to 350°. In a medium saucepan, melt butter over medium-high heat. Add mushrooms and onions, and sauté until mushrooms release moisture, about 5 minutes. Remove from heat.

Kids: In a 2-quart casserole dish, combine mushroom and onion mixture, rice, broth and salt. Stir to mix. Cover with a lid or with aluminum foil.

Adult: Place casserole in oven and bake for 45 minutes, or until broth has been absorbed. Remove from oven and serve.

Family Food Tip: Serve milk or another beverage in stemmed glasses — kids will feel "grown up."

LEMON RICE PILAF

This rice is a great side dish to serve with fish entrées.

1 tbs. butter
1 cup long-grain white rice
2 cups chicken broth
juice of 1 lemon
2 tsp. grated lemon zest

Adult: Melt butter over medium heat in a medium saucepan. Add rice and sauté until rice is translucent. Add broth.

Kids: Add lemon juice to rice and stir to mix. Cover and reduce heat to low. Simmer for 20 minutes, or until rice is tender. Add lemon zest, stir to mix and serve.

PARMA RICE

This is a great change-of-pace from serving pasta as a side dish.

3½ cups chicken broth
1 cup prepared tomato spaghetti sauce, such as Prego or Ragu
2 cups long-grain white rice
¾ cup grated Parmesan cheese
½ tsp. salt

Adult: Heat oven to 375°.

Kids: In a 2-quart casserole dish with a lid, combine all ingredients. Stir well to mix. Cover with lid.

Adult: Place dish in oven and bake for about 45 minutes, or until rice is tender. Serve immediately.

BROCCOLI CHEESE RICE

Servings: 4

Be sure to use converted rice in this recipe, or you will end up with a very mushy rice dish.

2⅔ cup water
1 cup converted rice
1 cup chopped broccoli
⅔ cup shredded cheddar cheese
½ tsp. salt
6 tbs. butter or margarine

Adult: In a medium saucepan, bring water to a boil over high heat. Add rice, stir to mix, cover and reduce heat to low. After 15 minutes of cooking, remove from heat and remove lid.

Kids: Very carefully add broccoli, cheese, salt and butter. Stir to mix.

Adult: Return saucepan to stove and cook for another 5 to 10 minutes, or until rice is tender. Serve immediately.

BACON AND EGG FRIED RICE

Servings: 4-6

This is a very Americanized version of Chinese-style fried rice — it may sound a bit strange, but it is really delicious. My kids call it "special rice."

½ lb. bacon
2 eggs, beaten
1 tbs. vegetable oil

5 cups cooked rice
1 tbs. soy sauce
½ cup cooked peas

Adult: Cook bacon until crisp. Drain on paper towels and cool. Drain all but 1 tbs. bacon fat from pan. Add egg and scramble until well done. Remove egg from pan and set aside.

Kids: Using your fingers, break bacon into tiny pieces. Set aside. Again using your fingers, break egg into small pieces. Set aside.

Adult: Heat oil over high heat in a large skillet or wok. Add cooked rice and stir-fry until rice begins to dry out a bit, about 10 minutes.

Kids: Drizzle soy sauce over rice and stir to mix. Add bacon, eggs and peas and stir to heat through. Serve immediately.

RICE CASSEROLE MONTEREY

Creamy and rich, this recipe is a very good use for leftover rice. It is not very spicy, but if you want an even milder version, use just half a can of green chiles.

2 cups cooked white rice
1 cup sour cream
1 cup shredded Monterey Jack cheese
1 can (4 oz.) chopped green chiles
½ tsp. salt

Adult: Heat oven to 350°. Butter the bottom and sides of a 2-quart casserole dish.

Kids: In a large bowl, mix all ingredients together. Scoop into casserole dish and level out the top.

Adult: Place casserole in oven and bake uncovered for 25 minutes, or until very hot throughout. Cool for 10 minutes before serving.

Family Food Tip: Display lighted candles on the table for no reason at all.

COUSCOUS WITH TINY VEGETABLES

Servings: 4-6

Couscous is a tiny, precooked pasta that comes from Morocco.

1 1/2 cups chicken broth
1 cup dried couscous
1/4 cup butter
1/3 cup finely chopped carrot
1/3 cup finely chopped celery
1/2 cup petite peas, frozen and thawed
1/4 tsp. salt

Adult: Heat chicken broth to boiling. Add couscous, stir, cover and set aside for 5 minutes. Heat butter in a small skillet over low heat.

Kids: Add carrot and celery to butter and stir until slightly cooked, about 5 minutes. Add peas and salt. Add vegetable mixture to couscous and stir to mix. Serve immediately.

CHINESE-STYLE NOODLES

Peanut butter on noodles? It makes a creamy base for the sauce, and blends Thai-style foods with Chinese.

½ cup smooth peanut butter
2 tbs. soy sauce
½ tsp. ground ginger
1 tbs. sesame oil
2 tbs. rice wine vinegar or water
8 oz. angel hair pasta
2 tbs. sesame seeds

Kids: In a small saucepan, mix peanut butter, soy sauce, ginger, sesame oil and rice vinegar.

Adult: Heat sauce over medium heat until smooth. Set aside. Cook pasta according to package directions and drain. Pour warm sauce over pasta.

Kids: Sprinkle sesame seeds over pasta. Using two large forks, gently toss pasta and sauce to evenly coat pasta and to distribute sesame seeds.

MAPLE-APPLE-GLAZED SQUASH

Servings: 6-8

Some people like their squash savory, but our family prefers it sweet. Use real maple syrup if you can.

1 butternut squash, about 4 lb.
½ cup butter, melted
½ cup maple syrup
½ cup apple juice

Adult: Heat oven to 400°. Cut squash in half; remove peel and seeds. Cut into about 2-inch cubes.

Kids: Place squash in a 9-x-13-inch baking dish. Pour butter over squash. In a small bowl, combine maple syrup and apple juice and stir. Set aside.

Adult: Place squash in oven and bake for 30 minutes. Pour apple juice-maple mixture over squash and stir to coat all pieces. Return to oven and bake for an additional 15 minutes, or until squash is tender and glazed.

SQUASH AND APPLE BAKE

Servings: 4-6

Squash and apples always taste great together. Here is an easy side dish to bake in the oven.

4 cups peeled, sliced butternut squash
1 large Granny Smith apple, peeled, cored, and sliced
6 tbs. brown sugar
2 tbs. butter, melted and cooled
½ cup apple juice

Adult: Heat oven to 350°.

Kids: Place about 1 cup of the squash in a 2-quart casserole dish. Place ¼ of the apple slices on top, and sprinkle with 1 tbs brown sugar. Continue until you have used up all squash and apple. Sprinkle with remaining 2 tbs. brown sugar and butter. Pour apple juice over all. Cover with lid or aluminum foil.

Adult: Place casserole in oven. Bake until squash and apples are tender, about 50-60 minutes. Cool for 10 minutes before serving.

TORTILLA STACKS

Servings: 4-6

These make an interesting side dish instead of rice or potatoes, when serving Mexican-style foods. They are most similar to enchiladas.

10 corn tortillas
1½ cups red enchilada sauce
1 cup shredded cheese
½ cup chopped olives

Adult: Heat oven to 350°.

Kids: Spread 2 tbs. of the enchilada sauce in the bottom of a round 2-quart casserole dish. Place a tortilla on top of sauce. Sprinkle 2 tbs. of the cheese over tortilla, and then 1 tbs. of the olives. Pour 2 tbs. of the enchilada sauce over olives and repeat with remaining tortillas until you have used them all. Top with remaining cheese and olives. Pour remaining sauce over olives. Cover with lid or aluminum foil.

Adult: Place casserole in oven and bake for 20 minutes, or until hot. Cool slightly, cut into wedges and serve.

ADULTS AND KIDS MAKE DESSERTS

LEMON PUDDING CAKE

This is a very old recipe that separates into two layers as it bakes: a cake on top, with a pudding sauce on the bottom.

2 eggs, separated
1 cup milk
1 tsp. grated lemon zest
1/4 cup fresh lemon juice
1 cup sugar
1/4 cup all-purpose flour

Adult: Heat oven to 350°.

Kids: Place egg whites in a large bowl. With an electric mixer on high speed, beat whites until stiff. Set aside. In another bowl, mix together egg yolks, milk, lemon zest, lemon juice and sugar. Add flour and mix well. Fold in egg whites. Pour batter into a 2-quart casserole dish.

Adult: Place casserole in oven and bake for 45 to 50 minutes. Cool for 10 minutes and serve warm.

CHOCOLATE HEAVEN PIE

This pie is for SERIOUS chocolate lovers only. I use a regular pie crust, but if you are really chocoholics, try a chocolate cookie crumb crust.

¾ cup granulated sugar
2 tbs. cornstarch
2 eggs
1 can (12 oz.) evaporated milk
1 cup fresh milk
2 tsp. butter
2 tsp. vanilla extract
2 oz. semisweet chocolate
2 oz. unsweetened chocolate
1 pie crust, 9-inch, baked
  and cooled

Kids: In a medium saucepan, stir sugar and cornstarch together until well mixed. Add eggs and mix well. With a wire whisk, add evaporated milk and fresh milk, and stir until completely blended.

Adult: Place saucepan over medium-high heat. Stirring constantly, bring mixture to a boil, about 10 minutes. Remove from heat and add butter, vanilla and both chocolates.

Kids: Stir mixture until chocolates have completely melted into milk mixture.

Adult: Pour chocolate mixture into pie crust. Refrigerate for at least 4 hours.

Family Food Tips: Finger cookies! Next time you make sugar cookies, don't use a cookie cutter. Trace your kids' hands or fingers onto the dough and then cut them out and bake them.

DOUBLE DELIGHT PIE

Servings: 6-8

My son Jon created this dessert — he loves s'mores, so he took his favorite flavors and combined them in a pie, with the ice cream holding it all together.

1 chocolate crumb pie crust
1 ½ quarts vanilla ice cream, softened
1 cup marshmallow cream
1 cup crushed graham crackers

Kids: Press ice cream into pie crust. Smooth marshmallow cream over ice cream, and sprinkle graham cracker crumbs on top. Place in the freezer until hard, about 2 hours.

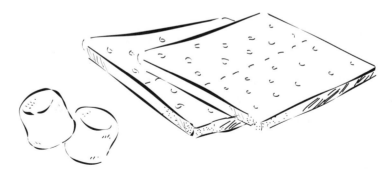

CINNAMON FLAN

A flan is delicious as is, but a bit of cinnamon gives it an authentic Mexican flavor.

¾ cup sugar
6 eggs
1 tsp. vanilla extract

½ tsp. cinnamon
2 cups milk

Adult: Heat oven to 350°.

In a medium saucepan over medium-high heat, stir ⅓ cup of the sugar constantly with a metal spoon until sugar melts and turns golden, about 6 to 8 minutes. Immediately pour sugar into a round 1-quart baking dish. Set aside.

Kids: In a medium bowl, mix together remaining sugar, eggs, vanilla and cinnamon. Pour in milk and beat well. Pour egg mixture into baking dish.

Adult: Place dish in oven and bake until a knife inserted in the center comes out clean, about 45 minutes. Remove from oven and cool on a rack. Refrigerate until cold, at least 2 hours.

To serve, run a knife around edges. Place a serving plate on top of the baking dish and invert. Cut into wedges and serve with syrup.

PEACHY BREAD PUDDING

Try topping this with a bit of whipped cream or vanilla ice cream.

4 slices bread
½ cup sugar
3 eggs
2 cups milk
½ tsp. salt
¾ tsp. ground nutmeg
1 can (15 oz.) sliced peaches

Adult: Heat oven to 425°. Butter the bottom and sides of a 2-quart casserole.

Kids: Tear bread into small pieces and place in casserole. In a medium bowl, combine sugar, eggs, milk, salt and nutmeg, and stir well to mix. Pour mixture over bread pieces. Cut peaches into bite-sized chunks and place on top of bread-milk mixture in casserole.

Adult: Place casserole in oven and bake for about 40 minutes, or until a knife inserted in the center comes out clean. Serve immediately.

KRISPY RICE S'MORE TREATS

Don't crush the graham crackers — you want small pieces, not crumbs!

3 tbs. butter
30 marshmallows
1½ cups crisp rice cereal
1 cup graham cracker pieces
1 cup chocolate chips

Adult: Spray a 9-inch square baking dish with nonstick spray. In a saucepan over medium heat, melt together butter and marshmallows until just melted. Set aside to cool slightly.

Kids: In a large bowl, stir cereal, graham cracker pieces and chocolate chips together Add melted, cooled butter-marshmallow mixture and mix well. With a spatula that has been sprayed with nonstick spray, spread in prepared pan. Cool.

Adult: Cut into 16 squares.

APRICOT BAKED CUSTARD

Servings: 4-6

Warm from the oven, this is sweet and creamy. A great winter treat!

1 cup canned apricot halves
4 eggs
1 ½ cups milk
½ cup sugar
1 tsp. vanilla extract

Adult: Heat oven to 350°. Spray bottom and sides of a 2-quart casserole dish with nonstick spray.

Kids: Cut apricots into bite-sized pieces. Arrange in casserole dish. In a large bowl with an electric mixer on medium speed, beat eggs until light, about 3 minutes. Add milk, sugar and vanilla, and mix on high for 1 minute. Pour mixture over apricots.

Adult: Place casserole in oven. Bake uncovered for about 25 minutes, or until a knife inserted in the center comes out clean. Serve immediately.

ALOHA POPSICLES

If you don't have a popsicle mold, don't worry. Just use little paper water cups, that you have lined with plastic wrap; you will need some wooden popsicle sticks to insert when they are just about firm. You can find popsicle sticks where kitchen gadgets are sold. Or you can use plastic spoons.

2 bananas
1 cup crushed pineapple with juice
1 cup sugar
1 cup whipping cream

Kids: Put all ingredients in a blender container and pulse until mostly smooth. Scoop mixture into popsicle molds and freeze until nearly firm. Insert sticks and freeze until completely firm.

Family Food Tip: Have dessert in front of the fire. Next time you have some cookies or other easy-to-eat dessert, gather everyone around the fireplace, turn out all the lights, and have a special finish to the meal.

SANTA'S FAVORITE
CANDY CANE ICE CREAM

We make this the day after Thanksgiving to start the holiday season off right!

4 medium-sized candy canes
2 eggs
1 cup sugar
2 cups half-and-half
2 cups heavy whipping cream

Adult: Place candy canes in a plastic bag.

Kids: With a kitchen mallet, pound candy canes into tiny pieces. Set aside.

In a medium saucepan, combine eggs and sugar, stirring to mix well. Add half-and-half and mix.

Adult: Place saucepan over medium heat. Cook mixture until it is thick and coats the back of a metal spoon. Do not let mixture boil. Remove from heat.

Kids: Add crushed candy canes to hot egg mixture. Stir well, until candy canes are mostly melted, about 2 minutes.

Adult: Pour mixture into a large container with a lid, cover and refrigerate to chill. When completely chilled, remove from refrigerator.

Kids: Add cream to candy cane mixture. Stir well. Pour into an ice cream maker and freeze according to manufacturer's directions.

CARAMEL BAKED APPLES

This hot apple dessert tastes like a caramel apple, but is far less messy to eat. Try it with vanilla ice cream or frozen yogurt on top.

4 Gala apples or other sweet baking apples
3 tbs. brown sugar, packed
1 tbs. butter, melted
10 small caramels, such as Brach's

Adult: Quarter and core apples, but do not peel. Heat oven to 375°. Spray the bottom and sides of a 9-inch square baking pan with nonstick spray.

Kids: Cut apples into large chunks and place in prepared pan. Sprinkle brown sugar over apples. Drizzle melted butter over brown sugar. Remove paper from caramels and place on top of all.

Adult: Place pan in oven and bake for 25 to 30 minutes. Remove from oven and cool for 5 minutes. Stir apples and sauce together to coat apples evenly. Spoon apples and sauce into individual dishes and serve.

FRESH FRUIT SOUP

Ok — this is really just a smoothie in a bowl, but it is fun to eat. It's fun to cut pound cake into tiny cubes, and pass the "croutons" around the table.

2¼ cups apple juice
3 cups fresh strawberries or peaches
2 tbs. sugar
whipped cream

Kids: Combine apple juice, strawberries and sugar in a blender container. Pulse until smooth. Pour into a large serving bowl, or into individual bowls, and top with a bit of whipped cream.

Family Food Tip: Celebrate achievements or milestones by letting the special child choose the main dish or the dessert for the meal.

ADULTS AND KIDS COOK
FOR THE HOLIDAYS

POTATO FINGERS

These oven fries are completely cooked, but still look white — that's how they got the name. Of course, dipping them in catsup is a must! Also, I tell the kids that it is a good idea to eat garlic on Halloween, in case there are vampires about...

6 large russet potatoes
6 tbs. vegetable oil
¾ tsp. garlic salt

Adult: Heat oven to 450°. Spray a baking sheet with nonstick spray. Peel potatoes.

Kids: Cut potatoes into ½-inch slices. Cut each slice into ½-inch-thick "fingers." As you cut potatoes, put them into a bowl of cold water to prevent them from discoloring.

Kids: When all potatos are cut, drain them and place them on a clean, lint-free towel, or on paper towels, and blot until dry. Put potatoes in a large, dry bowl and pour vegetable oil on top. Using your hands, mix potatoes until completely coated with oil. Pour potatoes and any remaining oil on baking sheet. Make sure potatoes are in a single layer.

Adult: Place baking sheet in oven and bake for 20 minutes. Remove sheet from oven, sprinkle potatoes with garlic salt and return to oven to finish baking. Bake for another 10 minutes. Remove from oven and place potatoes on paper towels to drain. Cool slightly and serve.

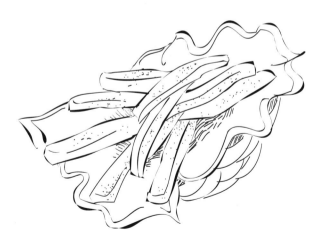

FULL MOON PIZZAS

These little pizzas aren't messy, so there is no need to worry about Halloween costumes getting dirty!

⅔ cup barbecue sauce
2 cups finely chopped cooked chicken
½ cup shredded mozzarella cheese
2 tubes (10 oz. each) ready-to-use pizza dough

Adult: Heat oven to 425°.

Kids: In a medium bowl, mix together barbecue sauce, chicken and cheese. Set aside.

Adult: Open pizza dough tubes for kids.

Kids: Stretch each piece of pizza dough to about 12 x 18 inches. Using a 2-inch round cookie cutter, cut out circles of dough. Spread 2 tbs. of the chicken mixture on half of the circles. Place remaining dough over chicken and pinch edges together very tightly. Place moon pizzas on a cookie sheet.

Adult: Place pizzas in oven and bake for 8 to 10 minutes, or until tops just begin to brown. Remove from oven and cool for 5 minutes. Serve immediately.

DEVILISHLY CHOCOLATEY CHOCOLATE CAKE

My son Stephen named this cake. It's so rich you don't need frosting.

1 pkg. (18½ oz.) chocolate cake mix
4 eggs
1 cup sour cream
½ cup chocolate syrup
½ cup water

¾ cup vegetable oil
⅔ cup mini chocolate chips
4 oz. white chocolate chips
2 tbs. shortening

Adult: Heat oven to 350°. Grease and flour a 10-inch Bundt pan or tube pan.

Kids: In a large bowl, combine all ingredients. Using an electric mixer, beat on low speed to moisten dry ingredients. Increase speed to medium and continue mixing for 3 minutes. Pour batter into prepared pan.

Adult: Place pan in oven and bake for 45 to 50 minutes, or until a toothpick inserted in the center of the cake comes out clean. Remove from oven and cool in pan for 20 minutes. Invert onto a wire rack and cool completely.

Melt white chocolate with shortening until smooth. Remove from heat.

Kids: Drizzle white chocolate over cake. Let chocolate harden before serving.

CALIFORNIA SUNSHINE JUICE

You can use fresh or frozen strawberries in this refreshing juice, so you can have it year-round.

3 cups orange juice
1 cup strawberries
2 tbs. honey

Kids: Put all ingredients into a blender container. Cover and blend until smooth. Serve immediately.

THREE CHEESE QUICHE

This is a great way to introduce your kids to quiche — it is rich and creamy, and will remind them of a cheese omelet.

1 deep dish pie crust, unbaked
6 eggs
2 cups half-and-half
1/3 cup shredded Swiss cheese
3/4 cup shredded cheddar cheese
3/4 cup shredded Monterey Jack cheese

Adult: Heat oven to 400°. Place unbaked pie crust in the oven and prebake for 10 minutes. Remove from oven and let cool. Reduce oven temperature to 325°.

Kids: In a large bowl, beat eggs. Add cream and cheeses, and stir well to mix. Pour mixture into partially baked pie shell.

Adult: Place quiche in oven and bake for 35 minutes, or until set, but still a bit "jiggly" in the middle. Remove from oven and cool for 15 minutes before serving.

FRESH PEACH JAM

Here's a simple way to prepare jam, without worrying about true canning. This lasts about 1 week when refrigerated.

4 cups sliced, peeled fresh peaches, about 1 ½ lb.
2 cups sugar
½ cup water
1 cinnamon stick

Kids: Mix all ingredients in a large Dutch oven or pot.

Adult: Heat to boiling over high heat, reduce heat to medium-low and simmer uncovered for about 35 to 45 minutes, or until thickened. Remove cinnamon stick and pour jam into a container with a tight lid. Store in the refrigerator.

BACON AND SAUSAGE EGG BAKE

Servings: 6-8 (or 2 very hungry dads!)

The dad in our family (my husband Chris) loves this topped with salsa. Serve a bowl of salsa on the side, and let your family decide.

$1/4$ lb. bulk pork sausage
$1/2$ lb. bacon, cooked
9 eggs
1 cup milk
$1/2$ cup shredded cheddar cheese

Adult: Heat oven to 400°. Spray a 9-inch square baking dish with nonstick spray. Crumble sausage into a small skillet and cook over medium-high heat until cooked through and just beginning to brown. Drain fat and set aside.

Kids: Break bacon into small pieces and put in baking dish. Place cooked sausage over bacon. In a large bowl, mix together eggs and milk. Pour egg and milk mixture over sausage and bacon. Sprinkle cheese over egg mixture.

Adult: Place pan in oven and bake for about 25 minutes. The center should be almost firm. Remove from oven and cool in pan for about 5 minutes; serve.

OVEN-BAKED HOME FRIES

Don't think "French fries" — these are a cross between hash browns and roasted potatoes. It's a simple way of preparing potatoes in the morning.

2 lb. russet potatoes
2 tbs. vegetable oil
1 ½ tsp. salt
2 tbs. butter

Adult: Heat oven to 400°. Spray a 9-x-13-inch baking dish with nonstick spray.

Kids: Slice potatoes thinly to make potato rounds. As you finish slicing potatoes, place them in a bowl of cold water to keep them from turning color. When done slicing, remove potatoes from water and blot dry with paper towels.

Pour vegetable oil into baking dish. Add potatoes, and using your hands, toss potatoes in oil to coat every slice. Arrange potatoes in an even layer in baking dish. Sprinkle salt over potatoes. Dot top of potatoes with butter.

Adult: Place dish in oven and bake for 45 to 60 minutes, or until potatoes are tender and light golden brown. Serve hot.

RASPBERRY SMOOTHIES

Servings: 4

My kids call this an "energy blend" or "power blend" because of all the nutritious ingredients. You can also use strawberries or blackberries if you prefer.

2 cups vanilla yogurt
1 cup milk
1 banana
1½ cups raspberries, fresh or frozen
½ cup ice

Kids: Place all ingredients in a blender container. Pulse on high until smooth. Serve immediately.

POTATO AVOCADO SALAD

Servings: 4-6

The flavors of guacamole mix with tiny red potatoes for a great summer salad.

2 lb. tiny new red potatoes, also called *creamers*
½ cup thinly sliced green onions
6 tbs. lime juice
½ cup vegetable oil
½ tsp. salt
2 tbs. fresh chopped cilantro
1 large tomato, coarsely chopped
1 large avocado, cut into small cubes

Adult: In a large pot, place potatoes and enough water to cover them. Bring to a boil over high heat, reduce heat and simmer until potatoes are tender, about 5 to 7 minutes. Drain and cool.

Kids: Mix together onions, lime juice, oil, salt and cilantro. In a large bowl, combine cooled potatoes, tomatoes and avocado. Pour dressing over all, and gently toss to mix thoroughly. Cover and chill until ready to serve.

RAZZLEBERRY LEMONADE

Servings: 6

I cheat on this recipe a bit because I use a lemonade frozen concentrate. If you want to spend a bit more time, make your own fresh lemonade; you will need about 7½ cups.

8 oz. fresh or frozen raspberries
1 can (12 oz.) frozen lemonade concentrate, thawed
6 cups water
¼ cup sugar, or to taste

Kids: Combine raspberries and lemonade in a blender container. Pulse until smooth. Pour mixture through a fine mesh strainer into a large pitcher. Press seeds and pulp down with a spoon, and discard anything that remains. Add water and stir to mix. Add sugar, one tablespoon at a time, stirring well after each addition. Taste after each addition of sugar, and adjust amount of sugar if desired. Cover and place in the refrigerator until very cold.

GODFATHER SANDWICHES

This is a sandwich you can't refuse! It is fun to make, and easy to tote along on a picnic. If you can't find mortadella, or if your family doesn't like it, you can substitute a good-quality bologna — have your deli slice it paper-thin.

1 round loaf sweet French bread, 1 lb.
2 tbs. olive oil
¼ lb. thinly sliced ham
¼ lb. thinly sliced salami
¼ lb. thinly sliced mortadella
¼ lb. thinly sliced provolone cheese
¾ cup shredded lettuce
1 medium tomato, sliced
1 tbs. red wine vinegar

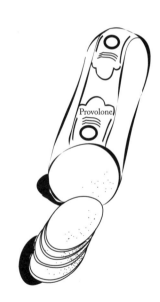

Adult: Cut a wide circle in top of bread loaf, about 1 inch in from the edge. Carefully lift off lid.

Kids: Pull out bread from lid and bottom and sides of loaf, leaving about a ½-inch-thick shell. Spread olive oil over inside of loaf and inside lid. Place half of the ham inside shell. Place half of the salami on top of ham, and top with half of the mortadella. Place half of the cheese on top of mortadella. Place lettuce on cheese and top with tomato slices. Sprinkle vinegar over tomatoes. Place remaining cheese on tomatoes. Layer with remaining mortadella, salami and finally, ham. Place lid on top and press down lightly.

Adult: Wrap loaf tightly in foil or plastic wrap and place in the refrigerator for 30 minutes. When ready to serve, cut into wedges with a sharp knife.

BACON-ROAST TURKEY

Servings: 10-12, 4 cups gravy

The bacon bastes your turkey as it cooks, and also makes a rich, flavorful gravy.

1 turkey, about 12-16 lb.
½ tsp. salt
1 lb. thick-sliced bacon
about 6 cups chicken broth
¾ cup all-purpose flour
2 tbs. Worcestershire sauce

Adult: Remove giblets from turkey and rinse cavities. Dry turkey inside and out with paper towels. Heat oven to 325°.

Kids: Sprinkle salt inside turkey. Place turkey breast-side up on a rack in a roasting pan. Place bacon over turkey, being careful not to overlap slices. Pour 1 cup of the broth into turkey cavity.

Adult: Place turkey in oven. Do not baste while bacon is on turkey. When bacon is very crisp, about 1½ hours, remove bacon from turkey and set bacon aside. Baste turkey with broth about every half hour until turkey is done, about 3½ hours to 4½ hours, or until a thermometer inserted in the thigh reads 180°–185°.

Remove turkey from oven and let stand for 30 minutes. While turkey rests, begin gravy.

Kids: Crumble bacon into tiny pieces. Set aside. In a small bowl, combine flour with 2 cups of the chicken broth. Stir until smooth. Add Worcestershire sauce and set aside.

Adult: Drain off any drippings and broth from turkey roasting pan. Pour into a measuring cup and add enough chicken broth to measure 4 cups. Bring broth and drippings to a boil over high heat in a medium saucepan. When at a full boil, gently pour in the flour-broth mixture, stirring constantly. Bring mixture to a boil, reduce heat to medium and cook for 5 minutes. If there are any lumps or bits of turkey fat or meat in gravy, strain gravy into another saucepan. Add crumbled bacon and bring gravy back to a full boil. Keep warm until serving time. Pass gravy with turkey.

APPLE CRANBERRY SAUCE

This is a nice change-of-pace from traditional cranberry sauce. It goes well with both poultry and pork dishes.

2½ lb. green apples, such as Granny Smith
¾ cup sugar
1 cup chopped fresh cranberries

Adult: Peel and core apples.

Kids: Cut peeled apples into chunks. Place apples into a large pot. Add sugar and cranberries, and stir to mix.

Adult: Cover pot and place on medium-high heat. Cook covered, stirring occasionally, for 45 minutes. Apples do not have to be completely cooked down. Remove from heat and cool.

CORNY PUDDING

This is halfway between spoonbread and creamed corn, and a very old-fashioned way to serve corn.

2 cups frozen whole kernel corn, defrosted
½ cup chicken broth
2 cups milk
1 tbs. butter, melted
3 eggs, beaten
½ tsp. salt

Adult: Heat oven to 300°. Spray the bottom and sides of a 2-quart casserole dish with nonstick spray.

Kids: In large bowl, stir together all ingredients until mixed. Pour into prepared casserole dish. Cover with a lid, or cover tightly with foil.

Adult: Bake for 45 minutes, or until pudding is firm and a knife inserted in the center comes out clean.

CHEDDAR MASHED POTATOES

Servings: 4-6

Here's an easy dish to make for holiday meals, because you can prepare it and then refrigerate it until you are ready to finish it off in the oven. It also travels well if you need to bring a potato dish to a potluck or as part of a large holiday gathering.

6 medium-large russet potatoes,
  peeled and quartered
¼ cup butter

¼ cup milk
1 cup shredded cheddar cheese
½ tsp. salt

Adult: Place potatoes in a large pot. Cover with water and bring to a boil. Cook until very tender, about 20 minutes. Drain well and return potatoes to pot. Spray bottom and sides of a baking dish or covered casserole with non-stick spray. Heat oven to 350°.

Kids: Using a potato masher or a mixer on medium speed, mash potatoes until smooth. Add butter and stir until melted. Add milk, salt and cheese, and stir until well mixed. Scoop potatoes into dish and cover with foil or lid.

Adult: Place potatoes in oven and bake for about 30 minutes, or until potatoes are very hot and cheese has melted. Serve immediately.

PUMPKIN BREAD PUDDING

You can bake this warm dessert while you eat dinner. I like to use the prepared pumpkin pie mix (usually found right next to the canned pumpkin) because it makes this dessert fast and easy to prepare.

8 slices bread (about 6 cups)
2 cups canned pumpkin pie mix
4 eggs
2 cups milk
⅓ cup sugar
½ cup raisins

Adult: Heat oven to 350°. Spray a 2-quart casserole dish with nonstick spray.

Kids: In a large bowl, tear bread into 2-x-2-inch pieces. In another bowl, mix together pumpkin, eggs, milk, sugar and raisins. Pour pumpkin mixture over bread and stir well to combine. Pour mixture into casserole dish.

Adult: Place dish in oven and bake for 45 to 55 minutes, or until a knife inserted in the center comes out clean. Remove from oven and cool for 5 minutes before serving.

MUSTARD MAPLE PORK ROAST

This may sound a bit fancy to serve to children, but both kids and adults like the sweet tart taste of the glaze, and, after all, Christmas should be special!

1 pork loin roast, 4-5 lb.
salt and pepper
apple juice
¼ cup Dijon mustard
½ cup real maple syrup

Adult: Heat oven to 425°.

Kids: Sprinkle pork on all sides with salt and pepper. Place meat in a roasting pan and pour ½ cup apple juice over it.

Adult: Place roast in oven and bake for 20 minutes. Reduce heat to 325°. Baste with pan juices (or more apple juice if needed) every 20 minutes. After about 1 hour, begin to check for doneness; an instant-read thermometer should register 120° when inserted into center of meat. When that temperature has been reached, remove meat from oven.

Kids: Mix together mustard and maple syrup. Brush or spoon mixture all over roast.

Adult: Return roast to oven and continue to cook until meat reaches an internal temperature of 150°. Remove from oven and let roast stand for 15 minutes. Pour drippings and pan juices into a measuring cup. Add enough apple juice to make 1 cup. Pour liquid into a small saucepan and bring to a boil. Strain and pass with meat.

CINNAMON MASHED SWEET POTATOES

I think everyone has had enough of candied yams with marshmallows. So here is a light and not overly sweet way to serve sweet potatoes this year.

4 sweet potatoes or yams, about 2 lb.   ¾ tsp. cinnamon
¼ cup butter   1 ½ cups applesauce

Adult: Place unpeeled sweet potatoes in a large pot and cover with cold water. Bring to a boil, reduce heat and simmer until sweet potatoes are very tender, about 20 to 30 minutes. Remove yams from water and cool just until easy to handle. Peel sweet potatoes and place in a large bowl.

Kids: Using an electric mixer, beat sweet potatoes until smooth. Add butter and mix well. Add cinnamon and applesauce and mix until smooth.

Adult: Spray bottom and sides of a casserole dish with nonstick spray. Heat oven to 400°.

Kids: Scoop potato mixture into prepared casserole dish. Cover with foil.

Adult: Place casserole in oven and bake until hot, about 20 to 30 minutes. Serve immediately.

PUMPKIN BREAD

This very moist, sweet bread can be served as a cake. It's delicious with a scoop of vanilla ice cream on top.

1 cup canned pumpkin
⅓ cup milk
⅓ cup vegetable oil
1 egg
1⅓ cups sugar
¼ tsp. ginger

1 tsp. cinnamon
¾ tsp. salt
¼ cup wheat germ
¼ tsp. baking powder
1 tsp. baking soda
½ cups all-purpose flour

Adult: Heat oven to 350°. Spray a loaf pan with nonstick spray.

Kids: In a large bowl, mix together pumpkin, milk, oil, egg, sugar, ginger, cinnamon and salt. In another bowl, combine wheat germ, baking powder, baking soda and flour. Pour flour mixture into pumpkin mixture and stir well to combine. Pour batter into prepared loaf pan.

Adult: Place pan in oven and bake for 50 to 60 minutes, or until a toothpick inserted in the center comes out clean. Remove from oven and cool in pan for 5 minutes. Turn out on a wire rack to finish cooling.

CHRISTMAS TRIFLE

The classic English dessert is beautiful when served in a glass bowl. This trifle is composed with vanilla cream, layered with slices of pound cake and drizzled with raspberry puree. The availability of frozen raspberries in December makes this dessert possible. Plan on making the vanilla cream early in the day, to allow enough time for it to chill.

VERY VANILLA CREAM
2 cups milk
1 cup half-and-half
¾ cup sugar
5 tbs. cornstarch
2 eggs
1 vanilla bean, split lengthwise

TRIFLE
2 cups raspberries
¼ cup sugar
2 cups whipping cream
¼ cup confectioners' sugar
1 tsp. vanilla extract
1 plain or lemon pound cake
1 cup raspberry jam

Kids: In a large saucepan, mix together all ingredients for *Very Vanilla Cream*, except for vanilla bean. Using a wire whisk, stir until completely smooth.

Adult: Place saucepan over medium heat. Add vanilla bean. Bring mixture just to a boil, stirring constantly. Reduce heat to low and cook until mixture is the consistency of thick custard, about 10 minutes. Remove from heat and remove vanilla bean. Scrape out interior of bean and add to cream mixture, stirring well to mix. Discard bean shell. Pour cream into a bowl and place a sheet of plastic wrap over top to prevent a "skin" from forming. Cool to room temperature and refrigerate to chill.

Kids: Place raspberries and sugar in a blender or food processor container and pulse until smooth. Set aside. Combine whipping cream, confectioners' sugar and vanilla in a large bowl. Using a mixer, whip into stiff peaks. Set aside. Cut pound cake into thin (1/4-inch-thick) slices. Spread raspberry jam on one side of each slice.

Assemble trifle: Place 1/2 cup of the vanilla cream in a serving bowl. Pour 1/4 cup of the raspberry puree over cream. Place a layer of pound cake over raspberry puree, jam-side up. Place 3/4 cup of the whipped cream over jam slices. Continue in this order: 1/2 cup vanilla cream, 1/4 cup raspberry puree, pound cake slices, 3/4 cup whipped cream, ending with whipped cream. Cover and refrigerate for at least 2 hours before serving.

CHOCOLATE MINT BROWNIES

These taste like a peppermint patty!

½ cup butter
2 squares (1 oz. each) unsweetened
    chocolate
¾ cup + 2 tbs. all-purpose flour
½ tsp. baking powder

¼ tsp. salt
2 eggs
1 cup sugar
1¼ tsp. peppermint extract

Adult: Heat oven to 350°. Spray a 9-inch square baking dish with nonstick spray. Heat butter and chocolate until just melted. Set aside to cool slightly.

Kids: In a large bowl, stir flour, baking powder and salt together. Set aside. In another bowl, beat eggs until well mixed. Add sugar and mix well. Add melted and cooled butter chocolate mixture, and mix well. Pour egg mixture into flour mixture and add peppermint extract; stir to mix. Spread batter in prepared pan.

Adult: Place pan in oven and bake for 25 minutes. Do not overbake. Remove from oven and completely cool in pan. Cut into 16 squares.

CINNAMON REFRIGERATOR COOKIES

These cookies are great during the holidays, because you can refrigerate the dough for up to a week, and have fresh hot cookies in just a few minutes.

1 cup butter, softened
1 ½ cups sugar
1 egg
2 ½ cups all-purpose flour

1 ½ tsp. baking powder
1 tbs. cinnamon
½ tsp. salt

Kids: In a large bowl, using an electric mixer, cream butter and sugar together. Add egg and mix. Add remaining ingredients and mix on medium speed for 3 minutes.

Shape dough into a roll of about 1 ½-inch diameter. Wrap in waxed paper or plastic wrap and refrigerate for at least 4 hours, or up to 1 week.

Adult: Heat oven to 375°.

Kids: Cut dough into ¼-inch slices. Place slices on an ungreased cookie sheet, about 1 inch apart. Put unused dough back into refrigerator.

Adult: Place pan in oven and bake for 8 minutes, or until edges are lightly browned. Immediately transfer from cookie sheet to a wire rack to cool.

OATMEAL MAPLE BARS

If your family likes maple syrup, these cookie bars will be a real treat. They are very fast to mix and bake, and taste great warm out of the oven.

½ cup granulated sugar
½ cup brown sugar, packed
½ cup butter
1 egg
½ tsp. baking soda
¼ tsp. baking powder
¼ tsp. salt
2 tsp. maple extract
1½ cups quick-cooking oats, lightly packed
1 cup all-purpose flour

Adult: Heat oven to 375°. Spray bottom and sides of an 8-inch square baking dish with nonstick spray.

Kids: In a large bowl, combine sugars and butter with an electric mixer on low speed. Add egg, baking soda, baking powder, salt and maple extract. Beat on medium speed until well mixed. Add oats and flour and mix on low speed until well combined. Scoop dough into prepared baking pan. Wet your hands slightly with water and press down on dough.

Adult: Place pan in oven and bake for 25 minutes. Cut into 16 squares while warm.

COCONUT SHORTBREAD

Makes 16

Even those who dislike coconut will enjoy this flaky cookie.

1 cup butter, softened
1/4 cup confectioners' sugar
1/4 cup granulated sugar
1 tsp. vanilla extract
2 cups all-purpose flour
1 cup flaked coconut

Adult: Heat oven to 350°.

Kids: In a large bowl, using an electric mixer on medium speed, cream together butter, sugars and vanilla until smooth. Add flour and coconut, mixing until a ball forms. Pat dough into an ungreased 10-inch springform pan.

Adult: Place pan in oven and bake for 20 to 25 minutes, or until light golden brown. Remove from oven and cool slightly. Remove outer ring from pan. Cut into 16 wedges while still warm.

INDEX

A

Aloha popsicles 97
Angel hair soup 29
Apple(s)
    caramel baked 100
    coffeecake 12
    cranberry sauce 120
    -maple-glazed squash 85
    and squash bake 86
    strata 18
Apricot baked custard 96
Avocado potato salad 114

B

Bacon
    and egg fried rice 81
    -roast turkey 118
    and sausage egg bake 111
Banana muffins 4
Bean, three, Tex-Mex salad 34
Beef
    chile Colorado 58
    chow mein 64
    herbed London broil 72
    meatballs olé 60
    Parisian-style short ribs 70
    slow-cooked pot roast 68
    stew, thieves' 66
    stew, walk-away 71
    tender meatballs 62
Beverages
    California sunshine juice 108
    raspberry smoothies 113
    razzleberry lemonade 115
Blueberry breakfast cake 16
Bread, pumpkin 127
Bread ring, Parmesan 20
Bread pudding, peachy 94
Bread pudding, pumpkin 123
Breakfast; see also Muffins,
    Scones
    apple coffeecake 12
    apple strata 18
    cake, blueberry 16
    crunchy granola 14
    lumberjack oatmeal pancakes
    17
Broccoli cheese rice 80

C

Cake
    apple coffeecake
    blueberry breakfast 16
    devilishly chocolatey choco-
    late 107
    lemon pudding 89
Caramel baked apples 100
Casserole, rice Monterey 82
Cereal, crunchy granola 14
Cheddar mashed potatoes 122
Cheese potato soup, Mexican 28
Cheesy potatoes 75
Cherry white chocolate muffins 6
Chicken
    creamy, and pasta 44
    full moon pizzas 106
    honey-grilled 50
    nuggets, earthquake 46
    "risotto" 43
    Spanish 51
Chile Colorado 58
Chinese-style noodles 84
Chocolate
    cake, devilishly chocolatey 107

H

Halloween
    devilishly chocolatey chocolate cake 107
    full moon pizzas 106
    potato fingers 104
Ham and potato soup 24
Herbed London broil 72
Honey-grilled chicken 50

I

Ice cream, candy cane, Santa's favorite 98

J

Jam, fresh peach 110
Juice, California sunshine 108

K

Krispy rice s'more treats 95

L

Lemon pudding cake 89
Lemon rice pilaf 78

M

Macaroni and cheese, classic 37

Maple oatmeal bars 132
Maple-apple-glazed squash 85
Meat
    bacon and egg fried rice 81
    bacon and sausage egg bake 111
    beef chow mein 64
    chile Colorado 58
    godfather sandwiches 116
    ham and potato soup 24
    herbed London broil 72
    meatball minestrone 24
    meatballs olé 60
    mustard maple pork roast 124
    Parisian-style short ribs 70
    pineapple pork chops 54
    pork chops with mushroom sauce 55
    slow-cooked pot roast 68
    tender meatballs 62
    thieves' beef stew 66
    tiny Texan ribs 57
    walk-away beef stew 71
    watermelon ribs 56
Meatball(s)
    minestrone 24
    olé 60
    tender 62

Mexican potato cheese soup 28
Minestrone, meatball 24
Mother's Day
    California sunshine juice 108
    fresh peach jam 110
    three cheese quiche 109
Muffins
    banana 4
    chocolate chip 5
    cinnamon 8
    cranberry 9
    white chocolate cherry 6
Mushroom sauce, pork chops with 55
Mushrooms with oven-baked brown rice 76
Mustard maple pork roast 124

O

Oatmeal maple bars 132
Oatmeal pancakes, lumberjack 17

P

Pancakes, lumberjack oatmeal 17
Parisian-style short ribs 70
Parma rice 79
Parmesan bread ring 20